CW01310862

THE BAPHOMETIC SCRIPTURES

As Revealed By
POPE MICHAEL C. HABORYM

INTRODUCTION

I am Pope Michael C. Haborym (Haborym being the surname I chose, upon becoming Pope). I founded the Church of Baphomet, and I am the head writer, and admin, of all matters, in the Church, and I work with the rest of the Clergy, in all Church matters, with the decisions being either decided by myself, or by voting.

I do not believe in God, and am entirely governed by the laws outlined, hereby, in this Gospel, and I believe that humanity would greatly benefit, from also being governed by these laws.

The Pope of this Church, is also a Priest, and a Bishop. To become Pope, you must be chosen by the current Pope, or by a mass vote throughout the Church, I, myself, defy this, due to being the sole founder of the Church. Throughout the Church, the Clergy are addressed, by default, as Reverend, but the individual can change this, some choose Father, some Elder, anything can be chosen, with respect to the actual rank/role they hold.

Our Church believes that pluralism in religion is fine, you can be a member of our Church/religion and another at the same time.

- Satan reading the scriptures, not really, he doesn't exist...

2022 – Church of Baphomet, as wrote by MCB
All Rights Reserved
Credit MUST be given if quoting this book
Fair use is at the discretion of the author, and whom is decreed, to speak on his behalf
churchofbaphometoffice@gmail.com

Dedicated to Lemmy, "He lived, why don't you…?"

THE GOSPEL OF

BAPHOMET

THE BOOK OF FIRE

1. I decree upon the realms, that should ye observe destructive adversity, ye should strive to remove it, and should the adversity strike ye directly, ye should surely destroy it.
2. I see not, race, I see - human, I see not, religious, I see - deceived. I am without the blindfold of prejudice, and such blindfolds should not be in existence, for they are nothing but true evil, and they are one the plagues of society.
3. Do ye not see this realm in a way other than the (so called) prophets tell you? They prove nothing to ye, but threaten ye with damnation, why should ye listen? Ye have blind faith, ye are lied to, ye are not at fault, but ye must learn.
4. I challenge the realms, the ones of blind faith, to read the things your book proclaims, and should ye see a thing that ye disagree with, to then think on that matter, for ye must believe it all to claim the truth of it, lest ye proclaim it also, ye must believe every letter, or ye shouldn't think about proclaiming to the realm, or ye are truly evil, one of the worst hypocrites of society, confining and scaring the peoples with threats of damnation, while not truly having faith in the book ye scare with, ye are evil.

5. The fire of hell is symbolic to the Church and we use it greatly, it represents the light Satanism can bring forth, if only ye knew.
6. Ye are deserving of literal fire, and tremendous pain, if ye harm the innocent or children, and should ye do this we would not inflict such punishment upon thee, but, we would not feel sorry for someone should it happen to them for harming the innocent. This is not barbaric, though it will be demonised as such, this is no different to any other claim, except ours, is rooted in truth and reason, ye see it not due to the blinding lies ye are indoctrinated with.
7. Hear, hear, I wish that ye would see this truth we are enlightened with, yet ye stick to these lies ye have been blinded with, what must ye hear or see to understand, I beg of thee to think, so thy life can be bettered.
8. I constantly proclaim that ye should believe whole heartedly and have proof of what ye believe, many search for truths but this criterium makes it simple, trust scientific, and proven facts, hereby I have gave ye relief, but ye thank me not, ye will not listen to what I hath said, instead ye will wait for someone of your religion to say the same thing, yet slightly twisted to fit the narrative ye desire, this is not a fact, but deception, ye see

it not, if only thou saw the truth, ye would benefit greatly.
9. Do not have blind faith, root it in fact, this is the most destructive thing man can do.
10. Harness the aggression ye have, why suppress such a great power ye hold? Ye deserve to realise your power, please try to.
11. Evil themes are good for thee, this releases the bad ye have in a safe way, without harming. Think music with evil themes, black masses, destruction, anything that releases that built up anger and bad in you without harming others.
12. Give unto others the anger they deserve, yet giveth love, should they deserve it.
13. Nothing should be inherently respected due to it being classed as religious, this is stupidity in its finest form, why should I respect something on the basis of somebody believing it?
14. I respect most animals more than humans, for they aren't held down by this stupidity witnessed by us, they haven't the illogical belief that a God who drowns almost everybody he creates, or that causes extremely painful disease or creates a world with suffering (that he can end), and still call that God merciful, ye are idiotic.
15. Do ye pray for better? Why not, just make it better? Ye pray to your mind, ye all believe in placebo effects when it suits ye, and believe its

God when it doesn't, or believe its the fault of humans if something doesn't fit your narrative, but if it does fit your narrative, its God, do you see how extremely demented this is, ye pray to yourself, should ye embrace yourself ye are smart but to believe its God, is (extremely) demented.

16. In this sheltered and biased world, your faith is the only thing that seems to get respect, this is ours, we hereby stand with a right to religious freedom, we, together, can achieve exactly what all major religions have, fairness. We can receive fair treatment from governments, we can demand it from people, from institutions and in every aspect of life where a law of religious rights has passed. To deny us this because of our beliefs or lack of belief in God is a crime worthy of fire, is it not?

17. Ye pay money for salvation, don't ye? Pay for a better home in heaven? You can not possibly think this is true. Ye should support the Churches that help you, but it should be optional, and also your idea to, and they shouldn't be vague on who it goes to, or what it is spent on. We are not vague, ask us, we will tell ye exactly where our money goeth. Destruction and abolition, is allocated for the Churches that demand the congregation's money, this is abhorrent, surely you see it?

18. To call a being ones enemy, you should hate them with every fibre of your being, otherwise ye dislike them, a Satanist will hold enemy for those he wishes to be destroyed, with no exceptions.
19. Hold closely your beliefs and proclaim them, this is encouraged due to the following law that we hold, ye must keep your beliefs objectively true, scientific fact in all cases.
20. Hail Satan, Hail Lucifer, Hail Baphomet! This proclamation is important, and through reciting it ye shall realise its true meaning, a way to express verse 11.

THE BOOK OF SATAN

1. Ye should free yourself from the false notions of right and wrong, and build your own, if ye should believe and choose to follow the teachings of this book, ye should have based your ideas upon these rules on what is right and wrong. Firstly, as long as your desire does not harm, ye should be free to do so. Secondly, ye should have consent from all parties involved, should it be an activity containing more than oneself. Finally, ye should be doing it for yourself and not others, and it should be based on your nature, and not the "so called" God's beliefs, remember, ye are your own God.
2. One's body is subject to nothing other than your own will, never have exceptions to this right, or ye hath forgone it.
3. Humanity needs guidance, and ye should get guidance based upon truth, not superstitious ideas. Why should ye get guidance from falsifiable lies, something ye can not attribute to the Gospel of Baphomet, for it claims not of anything other than morality, and of nature, and nothing of outgoing claims that need proving, nothing can be disproved in this, only disagreed with.

4. Peace is impossible to achieve because ye are diseased with a mind that causes evil forms of good, ye have greed, greed – applied in a way, without harm, is good. This can be applied to the majority of things major religions claim as sins, or bad, hence, why the first verse of the Book of Satan hath been revealed upon the realms, and ye.
5. Satan has been repeatedly labelled the bad one, yet think, ye are promised without any basis of proof, and it forces ye to live a life of fear and abstinence from all things enjoyable, surely this, is evil and bad?
6. Hath ye been deceived, hereby is an offer for ye to escape. Follow this Church, follow this Gospel, follow it for one week, and witness your life improve instantly, ye should agree, if not, it must be that ye are still holding the deceptions of the religions/God, in your mind, I beg that ye lose them, ye should realise that it is so bad.
7. Is it not foolish of ye to think ye don't have the rights to criticise? Is it not foolish of ye to think that ye don't also have the burden of being criticised? Ye must embrace this, it is the mark of freedom, ye should be mocked, this shall build ye stronger and generally better, embrace it.
8. Ye are you, not another, remember this.

9. Encourage your ego, ye should embrace it, ye should not do it to a point of being pretentious and annoying, but to a point where it aids your life and aims, and does not harm others (annoyance harms others).
10. Pacifism is idiotic, turning the other cheek is also, and many of these notions of 'peace' are wrong, and are instead an acceptance of being the weakling, the weakling is inherently – weak, nobody wants to be weak.
11. Satan is representative of all things that the human wants, anything can be Satanic. All have differing notions of what is Satanic, and it would be the opposite of the law of individualism in Satanism to attribute anything definite to Satan, that is the job of the Satanist.
12. God would be in debt to us if he existed, heaven should be the minimum he pays. I did not choose to exist, and I did not ask him for this, he is testing us against our wills, this is evil, if their notion of the devil or Satan is correct, he is it, vindictive, jealous, infanticidal, a terrorist with infinite victims, and misogynistic, delusional, stupid (due to the flaws in this badly designed place), and evil (alongside more titles), this list could last an entire book, its unlikely there are enough words to describe the abomination of a thing he would be.

13. The biblical Satan is misunderstood and vague, but from the general idea it gives of him, he would be an independent, non-conformist, self-defending and happy being, trying to save people from the idiotic and vindictive, jealous, infanticidal, a terrorist with infinite victims, and misogynistic, delusional, stupid, homophobic and evil, God.
14. Of God and Satan, as described in verses 12 and 13, who is the reasonable and correct being? Neither genuinely existing, but purely on hypothetical thinking, which do ye prefer?
15. Here I ask of thee to declare onto the realms, upon each corner of everything and to each atom, "Satanism represents kindness to they whom, under reasonable consideration, deserve it, as with love and all other things, deserve and receive, forgo and earn again, or never receive!" ye should be met with praise and questions on joining, yet due to the deception of the people that follow 'the divine' ye may be met with adversity, yet ye know what to do with adversity, destroy it.
16. Hath ye proclaimed the facts upon man? If you hath not, it is your duty, teach.
17. Is it not your duty, as a Satanist, to give help unto those in need? For helping those whom deserve it, is reasonable.

18. Is it not your duty to help those in danger, ye know the power of yourself, and should not doubt yourself, ye are powerful, beyond the amount most will ever know, though they should (hence the need to teach and proclaim), fear not, ye know if ye can face the adversary.
19. Give respect to your parents, elders and families, and whomever is of such a place in your life, this is not a commandment without exception, just a guidance for most.
20. Hail Satan, for through saying such, we may calm. Alike reciting prayers, ye shall receive the same feeling, or like meditating, ye shall receive more due to the release of your built up anger, and evil ye need to release (as stated in the Book of Fire – Verse 11).

THE BOOK OF LUCIFER

1. Lucifer represents humanity, rebellion against tyranny, the fact that it is perfectly fine to disagree with, and question, things.
2. Giveth unto your fellow man, should he be in need, for as ye do, should be how ye wish to have done unto ye, although, some people don't return thy favour, of those, cut them off, for ye need not, the arrogance, and do not need to associate with type of person that should do such an act.
3. Pray forth, for nothing, anymore. Rather, I say unto thee, make your actions – your prayers. For who wants meaningless words, spake unto himself, asking another to do his work for him, do it yourself.
4. How is it decided, that the human is any different, in what they deserve, that an animal, and how is it, that we look down on animals, as purely servants, this is idiotic, and we surely can see that we are more similar to they, than we are different, if only we could live in harmony, yet we can not, ye are too arrogant.
5. Many things that are decreed as bad, can be good, if only done in a good way, with it done the perfect amount, ye know not of this, due to ye being blinded by the ancient books, verily, I hope

ye see the truth I tell, and come forth, away from the blindness ye are cursed with, and unto this Church, surely, ye see this is better for ye.
6. Give unto those with strong faith, no punishments because of their faith, instead teach, teach that they are deceived, ye may be met with adversity, ye can destroy this with your actions, ye are decreed, therefore, to not stand idle, should ye be asked for your help in matters of religion, ye have the knowledge in this book, thus ye are able to help.
7. In books wrote by I, there may be repetition, or restating of the same things, this affirms the importance of such things, ye see it twice (or more) ye shall certainly do it, for it is good for ye, ye should see that.
8. Material is great for ye, for ye to see the fruit of what ye hath done, ye are made happy, ye are able to show what ye deserve and hath earned, ye are designed for this, yet they tell ye it is bad, how hath they come to this decision, it is they, trying to control ye, "giveth all your worldly treasures" for nothing, they tell ye its for something, but nothing hath, or will, come forth out of it. If only ye could see this, I weep for those who can not, ye are blinded.
9. Do not harm children among ye, in any way. And do not harm they who aren't harming ye, ye

should be equally respectful, or disrespectful, equally evil, or equally good.
10. Among ye, walks evil, they harm innocent people, for reasons, even they don't know (or have), they are the ones who deserve your wrath, ye should not be good to these, ye should not respect they, these are the enemy.
11. Do ye truly believe that we are superior to anything, humanity is the most idiotic and evil type of creature, to walk the Earth, among ye are the worst of the worst, for no reason, and this type of evil is not witnessed among any other being upon this place, wasps being the exception, yet even they hath a purpose.
12. Of thee I demand study, not faith, and of thee I demand ye research and agree with me, rather than believe and blindly accept, this is the difference betwixt Satanism and anything else, we are reasonable, they are not.
13. Indeed, ye have greed. Ye should change that greed, make it so it isn't greed to a negative extent, what defines negative is your decision, but I recommend ye halt the greed, it is better for ye.
14. Chant ye! Chant the infernal names, for through that, ye may harness the aggression, and ye will express the evil thoughts man has, why is it wrong to release the bad ye have in you?

15. Do ye even see the hypocrisy that ye have in your hearts? From the person who goes to Church on a Sunday or reads the Bible/prays every now and again, comes great hypocrisy, nothing more. Hypocrisy should be a crime!
16. Ye need comfort from your belief in heaven, I state here that if ye truly think about the fact ye believe that after we die, we go up to be judged by a man in the sky, who will punish people for eating the wrong meat, or missing Sunday mass or almost any of the sins that the Books say are bad, ye must be delusional. Think about what happens, imagine it, if ye still believe it, I declare ye a sheep, led to the slaughterhouse, for ye are the definition of stupid.
17. Aloud I ask of thee to speak this, if they truly wish to be a Satanist: "I call out to no God, I did not sin, I have been brought here against my will, and I have control, I denounce all religions that believe in God!" This is the affirmation ye must speak.
18. There is no heaven and no hell that ye go to after death. Heaven and hell are here upon this Earth, hell is to blindly follow rules that benefit nothing, and to believe in an idiotic book, and heaven is to denounce them and to follow worldly desires, ye must agree.
19. Repent to no God, repent to whom ye harm.

20.   Hail Lucifer, for he is the representation of whom the human wishes to emulate. With a life, living like the figure (and fictional life) of Lucifer, ye will have worldly pleasures, that many dream of. To forgo them, is surely a sin! Ye hath the power to live well, happy and fun. Ye should. Avoid drugs and any things that can cause ye to be controlled, then, ye shall be happiest, I promise!

THE BOOK OF BAPHOMET

1. Why do ye dedicate shrines to the image of Baphomet? For, it is a fantastic symbol, one that represents the beliefs, and stature, the Satanist strives to have. We are the Church of Baphomet because we use that image, it invokes feelings nothing else does, many are raised in lairs where such images are deemed evil, but we have opposing ideas of evil, and thus we use the images as a denunciation of such beliefs.
2. And many, upon this Earth, have caused death, and turmoil, wars and tears beyond count. Religions that follow the so called 'holy books', claim to forgive ye for these, but are nothing but lies to drag ye down, and to remove all worldly pleasures.
3. I deny not, that many rules in the 'holy books' are good for ye, that would be foolish and hypocritical of me, instead I say the notions of evil and good, and many of their rules, are indeed horrific, and stupid.
4. Behold, the crucifixion: an extremely painful way to be executed. Yet, many before, and after Jesus, died this way. I do not worship them, why worship him? Because a book tells me he was God's son? I see no proof.

5. Ye felt the holy spirit? I say ye felt your mind lying, as it often does, why did this person feel this religion's claim, and this person feel another religion's claim or God? Ye are relying on a placebo, ye shall die, and everybody will know that ye wasted your life on rules, that ye need not follow.
6. Do not follow something (a church) for the community! Exit your lair and look for a community elsewhere.
7. Adopt nothing, without proof.
8. Give exceptional attention to advancement in science, ye need to, for in proven science, comes truth, not in many-thousand year old, fiction books.
9. Ye need not pray, ye need to take action.
10. Respect nothing, that doesn't truly deserve respect, namely, the holy books, usually poorly written, contradictory works of fiction.
11. Do not join a religion that demands money, or worldly things, to follow! Ye should donate if ye wish to, but do not join if ye are forced to.
12. Make graven images, ye will be able to imagine what ye are thinking – better.=
13. Set your beliefs on paper, and then ye can live by your beliefs, ye need guidance, that is the good thing that religions bring, yet the guidance does not benefit ye, in them religions!

14. Satanism, is the religion of the intellectual.
15. Free yourself from what was once held as a sin. Ye will live better!
16. Have pride, ye are great, ye need not, to drag yourself down, ye do not need to kneel before God and apologise, ye hath not sinned!
17. Help your fellow man, if, the person deserves your help.
18. Affirm everything ye claim to believe, if ye cant, do not claim!
19. Hypocrisy and stupidity are the two biggest, and most evil, sins we have.
20. Hail Baphomet, Hail Lucifer, Hail Satan, Hail Fire, Hail Yourself!

THE GUIDE TO

PRACTICING SATANISM

THE PRACTICE OF SATANISM

WARNING!

The practice of Satanism is quite a personal thing. We (the Church of Baphomet) stay out of how you personally practice, the only exception being if you abuse the rules we have set forth, the main rule being that hurting anybody or anything (in a Satanic ritual) is a sin, and if you are found guilty, your membership will be revoked, INSTANTLY. No sacrifices are encouraged, and instead are outright banned, SACRIFICES ARE NOT SATANIC, BUT BANNED BY SATANISM!

THE ORDER OF THE BLACK MASS

The Priest will walk up to the altar, light all candles, and bow to the statue of Baphomet, then say "All Hail!" then the congregation will bow to the statue at the same time.

Priest - "Let us renew our denunciations"

All – "I hereby denounce all organised religions that believe in God, Gods or any supernatural being. I do not believe in a literal Satan, yet I see Satan as a being that I look up to, not a literal being, but an image that all should look up to, in the name of Baphomet, of Satan, and of Lucifer, I Hail, HAIL!"

Priest – "In the name of Lucifer, the light bringer, the representation of rebellion against tyranny on Earth, Lucifer represents the burning down of all things that we see as evil, Lucifer represents indulging in all of the seven deadly sins, as they instead are deadly sins, only, if you don't partake in them, for you wont be living. And now we recite the second verse of the book of Lucifer, Giveth unto your fellow man, should he be in need, for as ye do, should be how ye wish to have done unto ye, although, some people don't return thy favour, of those, cut them off, for ye need not, the arrogance, and do not need to associate with type of person that should do such an act. Together we say, HAIL LUCIFER!"

All – "Hail Lucifer!"

(Continues)

Priest – "In the name of Satan, we reaffirm the first verse from the Book of Satan. Ye should free yourself from the false notions of right and wrong, and build your own, if ye should believe and choose to follow the teachings of this book, ye should have based your ideas upon these rules on what is right and wrong. Firstly, as long as your desire does not harm, ye should be free to do so. Secondly, ye should have consent from all parties involved, should it be an activity containing more than oneself. Finally, ye should be doing it for yourself and not others, and it should be based on your nature, and not the "so called" God's beliefs, remember, ye are your own God. Together, we will say, HAIL SATAN!"

All – "Hail Satan!"

(Continues)

Priest – "In the name of Baphomet, we will remember why we dedicate shrines to he, and why we name our church – the Church of Baphomet, by reading the first verse of the Book of Baphomet. Why do ye dedicate shrines to the image of Baphomet? For it is a fantastic symbol, that represents the beliefs and stature the Satanist strives to have. We are the Church of Baphomet because we use that image, it invokes feelings nothing else does, many are raised in lairs where such images are deemed evil, but we have opposing ideas of evil, and thus we use the images as a denunciation of such beliefs. Together we say Hail Baphomet!"

All – "Hail Baphomet!"

Priest – "To end our mass, we shall say Ave Satanas!"

All – "Ave Satanas)

(Play Satanic Hymn As All Exit)

THE SATANIC HOLIDAYS/HOLY DAYS

Satanism has many holidays, all of which should be observed, this is because Satanism is based upon imagery and feeling what you speak and believe.

The most important of all Holidays in Satanism, is ones own birthday. There is also the day of 'Dies Satanae', which is the day of Satan, and we decided to hold it on December 25th as this allows Satanists to keep the tradition of that day, as this comes natural to most people.

We also hold the day of Halloween quite special, this is the day for all to embrace the brilliance of darkness and Satanic imagery, and is also a day to try end your fears, this should be held in high regard, and the Satanist should try perform, or attend, a black mass on this day (if possible).

A very important and solemn day for Satanists is Hexennacht, this day is to honour those affected by superstition, and the Satanic Panic, and the witch hunts, this day is held on April 30th.

THE 8 SATANIC COMMANDMENTS

1 – Do not harm living things, unless for defence, especially not children!

2 – Ignore the seven deadly sins, and observe using them all, they are not harmful unless done in excess.

3 – Do not be hypocritical

4 – Do not be stupid

5 – Be a good person

6 – We believe in taking responsibility for things we do, instead of blaming it on imaginary angels and demons

7 – We believe in facts

8 – Do not make sexual (or any kind of) advances on non-inviting beings

These are designed to be acceptable by all, and should you read these, and agree, I ask you, with good intention in my heart, to read the rest of this book, I whole-heartedly believe you will benefit from them.

SATANISM AND THE BELIEF IN GOD

Some branches of Satanism are theistic, but we do not accept that as Satanism. In our definition Satanism is the opposition to religions that believe in God, superstition, dogmatic and pointless rules, tyranny, the lack of freedom of religion (ie. anything that punishes apostasy, Islam being a major example of this), the lack of sexual freedom, and the practice of ignoring scientific fact due to wanting to believe the religion they are scared into.

Satanism is atheistic! That needed to be stated clearly...

So, no, we do not worship Satan, or anything. Saying "Hail Satan" is merely a way to express that we hail, and admire, the figure of Satan.

Satanism is the expression of individualism. Satanism is more the belief in oneself as a God of himself, than the belief in a God.

SELLING YOUR SOUL

Nope, you can't...

You have no soul to sell!

Satanism is not going to bring you riches and power, we are not the dark side (as seen in movies). You do not become a dark lord when you become a member of the Church of Baphomet! You are the same person.

You do not become a Satanist for any reason other than to identify as a Satanist, and to show your support for our Church.

In addition to everything else, you do not even need to join our Church to be a Satanist, if you agree, you likely are, but (as stated in the Book of Fire Verse 4) only if you agree with everything stated.

And, to become a member, your main thing to do (other than signing up) is to utter, or merely agree with, the denunciation.

THE DENUNCIATION

"I hereby denounce all organised religions that believe in God, Gods, or any supernatural being. I do not believe in a literal Satan, yet I see Satan as a being that I look up to, not a literal being, but an image that all should look up to, in the name of Baphomet, of Satan, and of Lucifer, I say Hail Satan."

LEADING A

SATANIC LIFE

THE DUTIES OF THE SATANIST

FIGHT

- To fight tyranny
- To fight for a better world
- To fight for rights
- To fight against abuse
- To fight for the weak

TEACH

- To teach science
- To teach the falsehoods religions promote
- To teach that religions lie

RESIST

- To resist anything that affects people negatively
- To resist anti-freedom of religion laws
- To resist and refute God
- To resist any laws that infringe on the rights of the people

LIVE

- Live how you want

THE SATANIC SINS

Harming innocent people

Harming children

Stupidity

Ignoring facts and science

Not refuting obvious lies and idiotic claims

Changing yourself in front of other/Don't be two faced

Abstaining from the 7 Deadly sins

Cheating on a spouse or partner

Lying, with the exception of white lies (some lies are good)

Not doing things you love

Framing others

Imposing uninvited upon others

THE

ENOCHIAN KEYS

The Enochian Keys are commonly held in high regard by Satanists. These are of no special relevance to us, but are recommended reading for Satanists, you should have read them. They have quite an interesting history that I recommend you research, they are a lot more about magic than I like, but they are still good to read. *If you wish, you could change God for Satan, and use them in Black Masses.*

I reign over you, says the God of Justice, in power exalted above the firmaments of wrath: in whose hands the Sun is as a sword and the Moon as a through thrusting fire: which measures your garments in the midst of my vestures, and trussed you together as the palms of my hands: whose seats I garnished with the fire of gathering, and beautified your garments with admiration. To whom I made a law to govern the holy ones and delivered you a rod with the ark of knowledge. Moreover you lifted up your voices and swore obedience and faith to him that lives and triumphs, whose beginning is not, nor end can not be, which shines as a flame in the midst of your palace, and reigns amongst you as the balance of righteousness and truth. Move, therefore, and show yourselves: open the Mysteries of your Creation: Be friendly unto me: for I am the servant of the same your God, the true worshipper of the Highest.

Can the wings of the winds understand your voices of wonder, O you the second of the first, whom the burning flames have framed within the depth of my Jaws; whom I have prepared as Cups for a Wedding, or as the flowers in their beauty for the Chamber of righteousness. Stronger are your feet than the barren stone, and mightier are your voices than the manifold winds. For you are become a building such as is not, but in the mind of the All Powerful. Arise, says the First: Move therefore unto his Servants: Show yourselves in power: And make me a strong seething: for I am of him that lives for ever.

Behold, says your god, I am a Circle on whose hands stand 12 Kingdoms: Six are the seats of Living Breath: the rest are as sharp sickles or the horns of death, wherein the Creatures of your earth are to are not, except mine own hand which sleep and shall rise. In the first I made you Stewards and placed you in 12 seats of government. giving unto every one of you power successively over 456, the true ages of time: to the intent that from your highest vessels and the corners of your governments you might work my power, pouring down the fires of life and increase continually on the earth: Thus you are become the skirts of Justice and Truth. In the Name of the same your God, lift up, I say, your selves. Behold his mercies flourish and Name is become mighty amongst us. In whom we say: Move, Descend, and apply yourselves unto us, as unto the partakers of the Secret Wisdom of your Creation.

I have set my feet in the south and have looked about me, saying, are not the Thunders of increase numbered 33 which reign in the Second Angle? under whom I have placed 9639 whom none hath yet numbered but one, in whom the second beginning of things are and wax strong, which also successively are the number of time: and their powers are as the first 456. Arise, you Sons of pleasure, and visit the earth: for I am the Lord your God which is, and liveth. In the name of the Creator, Move and show yourselves as pleasant deliverers, That you may praise him amongst the sons of men.

The mighty sounds have entered in your 3rd Angle and are become as olives in your olive mount, looking with gladness upon the earth and dwelling in the brightness of the heavens as continual comforters. Unto whom I fastened pillars of gladness 19 and gave them vessels to water the earth with her creatures: and they are the brothers of the first and second and the beginning of their own seats which are garnished with continually burning lamps 69636 whose numbers are as the first, the ends, and your contents of time. Therefore come you and obey your creation: visit us in peace and comfort: Conclude us as receivers of your mysteries: for why? Our Lord and Mr is all One.

The spirits of your 4th Angle are Nine, Mighty in the firmament of waters: whom the first has planted a torment to the wicked and a garland to the righteous: giving unto them fiery darts to winnow the earth and 7699 continual Workmen whose courses visit with comfort the earth and are in government and continuance as the second and the third. Wherefore hearken unto my voice: I have talked of you and I move you in power and presence: whose Works shall be a song of honour and the praise of your God in your Creation.

The East is a house of virgins singing praises amongst the flames of first glory wherein the Lord hath opened his mouth: and they are become 28 living dwellings in whom the strength of man rejoices, and they are apparelled with ornaments of brightness such as work wonders on all creatures. Whose Kingdoms and continuance are as the Third and Fourth Strong Towers and places of comfort, The seats of Mercy and Continuance. O you Servants of Mercy: Move, Appear: sing praises unto the Creator and be mighty amongst us. For to this remembrance is given power and our strength waxes strong in our Comforter.

The Midday, the first, is as the third heaven made of Hyacinth Pillars 26: in whom the Elders are become strong which I have prepared for my own righteousness says the Lord: whose long continuance shall be as bucklers to the stooping Dragon and like unto the harvest of a Widow. How many are there which remain in the glory of the earth, which are, and shall not see death, until this house fall and the Dragon sink? Come away, for the Thunders have spoken: Come away, for the Crowns of the Temple and the coat of him that is, was, and shall be crowned, are divided. Come, appear to the terror of the earth and to our comfort and of such as are prepared.

A mighty guard of fire with two edged swords flaming, which have Vials 8 of Wrath for two times and a half: whose wings are of wormwood and of the marrow of salt, have settled their feet in the West and are measured with their Ministers 9996. These gather up the moss of the earth as the rich man doth his treasure: cursed are they whose iniquities they are in their eyes are millstones greater then the earth, and from their mouths run seas of blood: their heads are covered with diamond, and upon their heads are marble sleeves. Happy is he on whom they frown not. For why? The God of righteousness rejoices in them! Come away, and not your Vials, for the time is such as requires comfort.

The Thunders of Judgment and Wrath are numbered and are harboured in the North in the likeness of an oak, whose branches are Nests 22 of Lamentation and Weeping laid up for the earth, which burn night and day: and vomit out the heads of scorpions and live sulphur mingled with poison. These are the Thunders that 5678 times in ye 24th part of a moment roar, with a hundred mighty earthquakes and a thousand times as many surges, which rest not nor know any echoing time between. One rock brings forth 1000, even as the heart of man does his thoughts. Wo, Wo, Wo, Wo, Wo, Wo, yea Wo be to the earth! For her iniquity is, was and shall be great! Come away: but not your noises.

The Mighty Seat groaned and they were 5 thunders which flew into the East: and the Eagle spoke and cried with a loud voice, Come away: and they gathered themselves together and became the house of death of whom it is measured and it is as they are, whose number is 31. Come away, for I have prepared for you. Move therefore, and show yourselves: open the Mysteries of your Creation: be friendly unto me: for I am the servant of the same your God, the true worshipper of the Highest.

O you that reign in the South and are 28, The Lanterns of Sorrow, bind up your girdles and visit us. Bring down your train 3663 that the Lord may be magnified, whose name amongst you is Wrath. Move, I say, and show yourselves: open ye Mysteries of your Creation: be friendly unto me: for I am the servant of the same your God, the true worshipper of the Highest.

O you swords of the South which have 42 eyes to stir up the wrath of sin, making men drunken which are empty. Behold the promise of God and his power which is called amongst you a Bitter Sting. Move and show yourselves: open the Mysteries of your Creation: be friendly unto me: for I am the servant of the same your God, the true worshipper of the Highest.

O you sons of fury, the daughters of the lust, which sit upon 24 seats, vexing all creatures of the earth with age, which have under you 1636: behold the Voice of God, the promise of him which is called amongst you Fire or Extreme Justice. Move and show yourselves: open the Mysteries of your Creation: be friendly unto me: for I am the servant of the same your God, the true worshipper of the Highest.

O you the governor of the first flame under whose wings are 6739 which weave the earth with dryness: which knows the great name Righteousness and the Seal of Honour. Move and show yorselves: open the Mysteries of your Creation: be friendly unto me: for I am the servant of the same your God, the true worshipper of the Highest.

O you second flame, the house of Justice, which has your beginning in glory and shall comfort the just: which walks on the earth with feet 8763 that understand and separate creatures: great are you in the God of Stretch Forth and Conquer. Move and show yourselves: open the Mysteries of your Creation: be friendly unto me: for I am the servant of the same your God, the true worshipper of the Highest.

O you third flame whose wings are thorns to stir up vexation and hast 7336 Lamps Living going before you, whose God is Wrath in Anger, gird up your loins and hearken. Move and show yourselves: open the Mysteries of your Creation: be friendly unto me: for I am the servant of the same your God, the true worshipper of the Highest.

O you mighty Light and burning flame of comfort which opens the glory of God to the centre of the earth, in whom the Secrets of Truth 6332 have their abiding, which is called in thy kingdom Joy and not to be measured: be you a window of comfort unto me. Move and show yourselves: open the Mysteries of your Creation: be friendly unto me: for I am the servant of the same your God, the true worshipper of the Highest.

O you heavens which dwell in the {Number of Aether, eg First Ayre}, the mighty in the parts of the Earth, and execute the Judgment of the Highest! To you it is said, Behold the face of your God, the beginning of comfort, whose eyes are the brightness of the heavens: which provided you for the government of the Earth and her unspeakable variety, furnishing you with a powerful understanding to dispose all things according to the providence of Him that sits on the Holy Throne, and rose up in the beginning, saying: the Earth let her be governed by her parts and let there be division in her, that the glory of her may be always drunken and vexed in itself. Her course, let it run with the heavens, and as a handmaid let her serve them. One season let it confound another, and let there be no creature upon or within her the same: all her members let them differ in their qualities, and let there be no one creature equal with another: the reasonable Creatures of the Earth let them vex and weed out one another, and the dwelling places let them forget their names: the work of man, and his pomp, let them be defaced: his buildings let them become caves for the beasts of the field. Confound her understanding with darkness.

For why? It repents me I made Man. One while let her be known and another while a stranger: because she is the bed of a Harlot, and the dwelling place of Him that is Fallen. O you heavens arise: the lower heavens underneath you, let them serve you! Govern those that govern: cast down such as fall! Bring forth with those that increase, and destroy the rotten! No place let it remain in one number: add and diminish until the stars be numbered! Arise, Move, and Appear before the Covenant of his mouth, which he has sworn unto us in his Justice. Open the Mysteries of your Creation: and make us partakers of Undefiled Knowledge.

THE

GALLERY

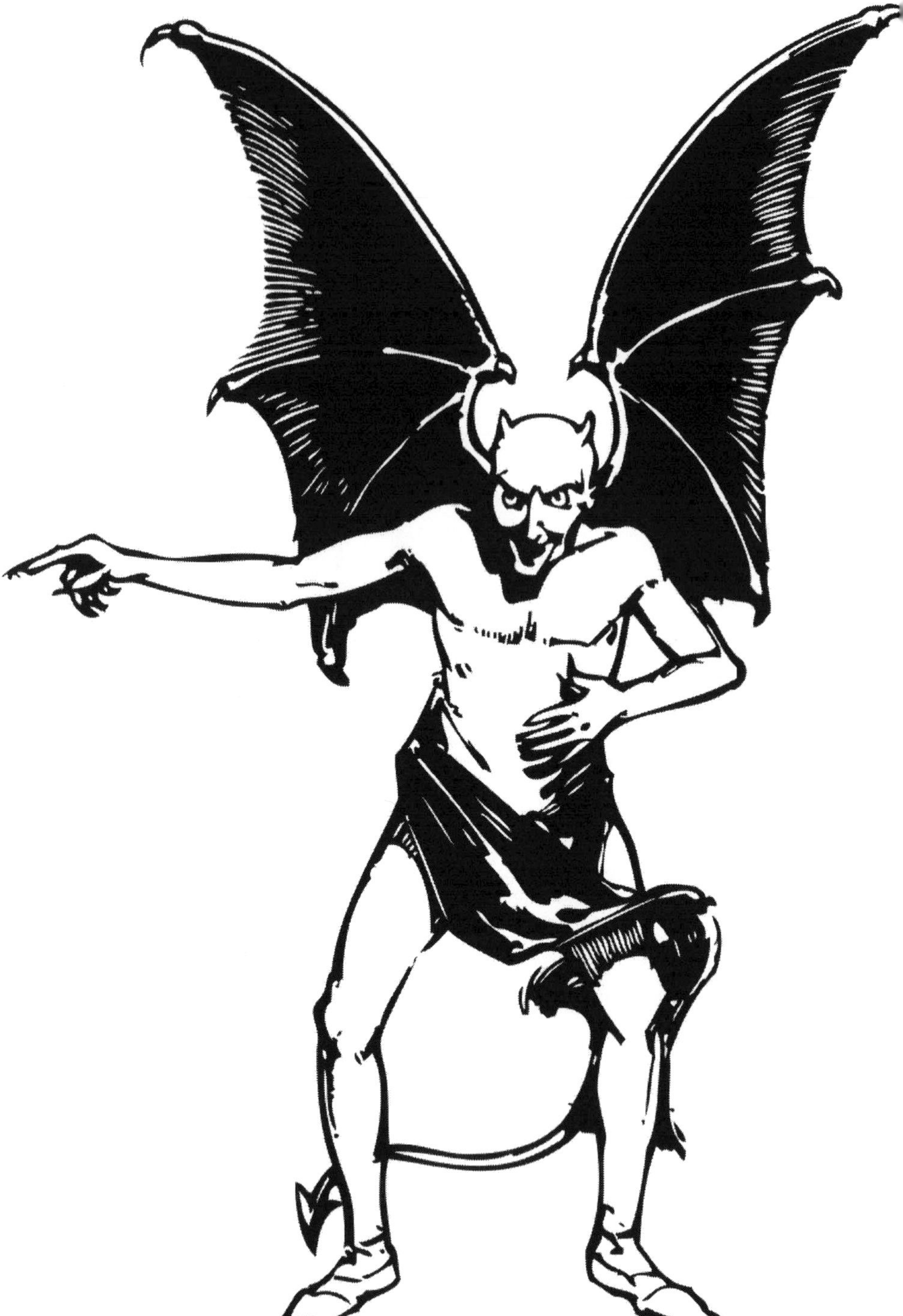

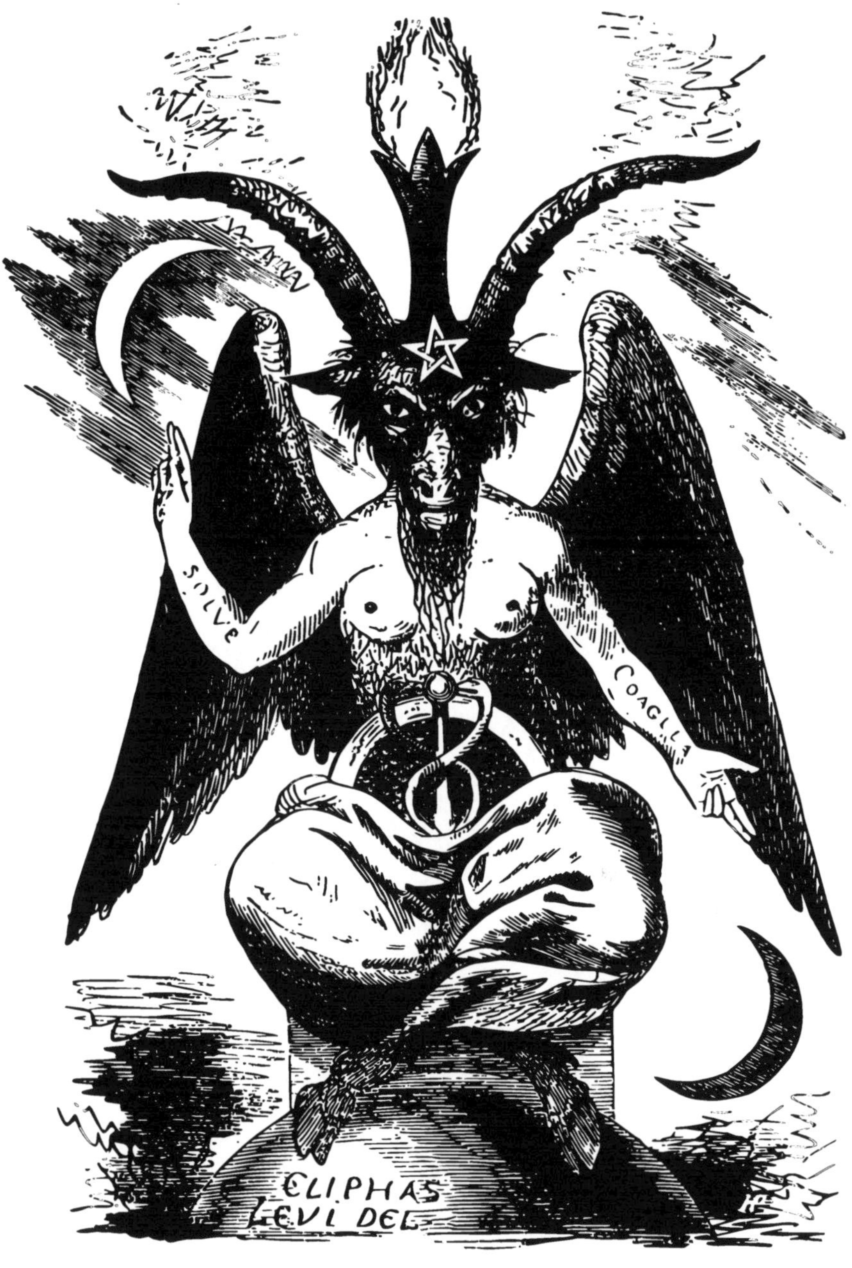
SOLVE
COAGULA
ELIPHAS
LEVI DEL

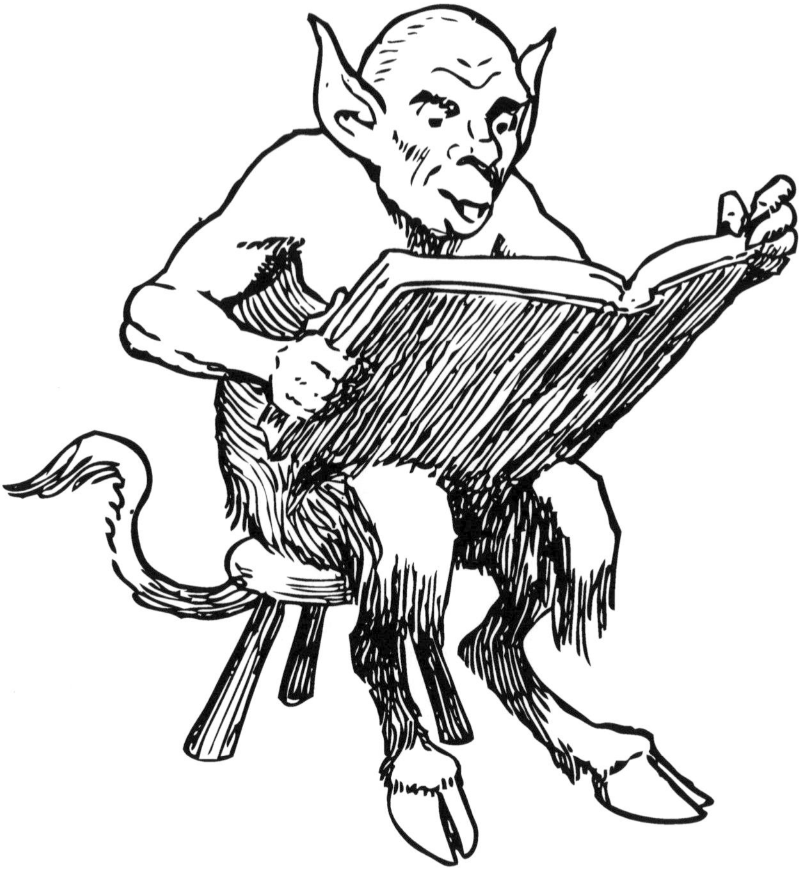

RECOMMENDED READING

The Satanic Bible – Anton LaVey

The God Delusion – Richard Dawkins

The Bible – Some Random People Thousands of Years Ago

The Book of Mormon – Joseph Smith

The Quran – Muhammad's Scribes Around 200 Years After He Died

The Guru Granth Sahib (a holy book, that I actually have a very small amount, of problems with)

And I ask you read this book again, and share it (preferably tell them to buy a copy for themselves)

HAIL SATAN

Email Us, for a way to join!

churchofbaphometoffice@gmail.com

Be A Good Person.

Printed in Great Britain
by Amazon

4a25b160-69ce-4bb9-bdbc-1f71c9616a96R01